Among the Odds & Evens

A Tale of Adventure

Priscilla Turner

Pictures by
Whitney Turner

Farrar Straus Giroux

New York

For our father and his love of imaginary numbers

Distributed in Canada by Douglas & McIntyre Ltd.
Color separations by Hong Kong Scanner Arts
Printed and bound in the United States of America by Worzalla
First edition, 1999

Library of Congress Cataloging-in-Publication Data
Turner, Priscilla.
    Among the odds & evens : a tale of adventure / Priscilla Turner ;
pictures by Whitney Turner.
        p.   cm.
    Summary: When X and Y crash in the land of Wontoo, they cannot
understand how the Numbers live the way they do, until they not only
get used to it, but decide they want to stay in Wontoo.
    ISBN 0-374-30343-6
    [1. Numbers Natural—Fiction.   2. Alphabet—Fiction.   3. Manners and
customs—Fiction.]   I. Turner, Whitney, ill.   II. Title.
PZ7.T8575Am   1999
[E]—dc21   98-8055

Far, far away, in a whole other part of the world, two Adventurers set off from the Land of Letters in their Aerocycle.

They had been trekking for a year and a day when out of the blue they developed technical difficulties.

X and Y crash-landed in the middle of what seemed to be a village.

X leapt out of the broken Aerocycle and was approached by curious villagers. "Welcome to the Kingdom of Wontoo," one of them said.

X whipped out his notebook and pen to write down the name on his List of Discoveries. "Uncharted on our maps," he said. "And what's the name of this range?" He gestured toward the towering peaks they'd cycled over.

"The Numeris Mountains," answered another villager politely.

"Also uncharted," announced X, adding the mountain range to his List.

The Wontoois invited X and Y to set up camp right in the middle of Wontoo.

After many long hours of work on the injured Aerocycle, X and Y set aside a day to explore the village.

"My word," said X to Y. "I observe that Wontoois appear to be divided into two distinct groups!"

"Why, yes!" retorted Y. "Some Wontoois are orderly and predictable. In short, *even*-tempered."

"But notice," continued Y, "that other Wontoois, by way of contrast, positively revel in peculiar dress and behavior —one might even call them quite *odd*!"

X nodded. "Indeed, 'How odd!' seems to be the highest compliment they can bestow on one another!"

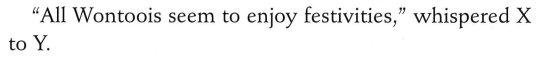

"All Wontoois seem to enjoy festivities," whispered X to Y.

"Well, yes," agreed Y, "although I sense Odd Wontoois are often bored at Even functions."

"Do you think," said Y excitedly, "that this is how some Odds and Evens meet and fall in love?"
"I do!" concurred X emphatically.

That evening, as they dined, Y dropped his fork with a loud clatter. "By Jove, X!" he said. "How did we not notice this earlier?"

"Notice what, Y?" asked X, following his companion's gaze.

Y pointed. "Evens have only Even children. Yet two Odd parents also seem to have only Even children."

"Y, you are right!" rejoined X excitedly as he pointed to another family. "It is only when one parent is Odd and the other is Even that we see Odd children. Most unletter-like!" X frowned. "We must investigate further!"

X, a straightforward sort of fellow, decided to take the bull by the horns. "Why," X asked a startled husband and wife, "don't you Odds ever have Odd children like yourselves?"

The Odd couple answered politely—even though they privately considered the Letters rude—"It's just a fact of Number life."

"Well," continued X, "it makes no sense to us. In the Land of Letters, A's have a's, B's have b's. Everyone has children like himself. And that is how it should be."

"Hear, hear!" chimed in Y, although he wasn't really listening.

"I'm sorry if our ways offend you," 3 said politely but firmly, "but there's nothing odd about Even children being a product of an Odd pair. Even you must see that."

"How ghastly!" fretted X later that night. "The behavior of these Numbers. Not at all the sort of thing we're used to! I'll be glad when our Aerocycle is repaired and we can return to Civilization!"

Y and X liked to think of themselves as Letters of the World, but when it came right down to it, they were quite provincial. The customs they enjoyed in the Land of Letters were the only ones they were comfortable with.

Beginning the next day, every spare moment not devoted
to repairing the ailing Aerocycle was spent trying to make
the Wontoois see things their way.

The Letters didn't realize that the excellent Wontooi
custom of Good Manners was the only thing that kept the
Numbers from calling them rude, interfering fools.

One day the Numbers held a secret town meeting. "I know," fumed a 4, "that I shouldn't let Y and X annoy me, but they do! Imagine them telling us how to raise our children!"

"It's worse than that!" added a 5. "They're telling us what children to *have*!"

"And how hard is an Aerocycle to fix?" groused a 6. "Shouldn't they be done by now?"

Finally, the Lord High Mayor, who was truly wise, spoke. "I know it is difficult, but do not allow these Aerocycle-pedaling Letters to disrupt the harmony of our village. Trust me, it will all add up in the end."

"The stubbornness of these Numbers!" complained X to Y. "Have you ever seen such an unwillingness to adapt to new ideas!?" Y shook his head sorrowfully. "Wait until they hear about this at the Royal Letters Society!"

Despite their opinions, they saw no reason to deprive themselves of the excellent Wontooi hospitality.
X considerably enjoyed Even art shows. (He had always loved symmetry, he now realized.)

And Y particularly liked Odd nightlife, and more than one evening found himself gavotting and galloping till dawn at Club 31.

Many months had passed since the day the Letters had crash-landed in the village of Wontoo. There really seemed to be no logical reason the Aerocycle wasn't up and flying and the Letters on their way.

No reason, that is, but one . . .

"What are you doing here?" asked a startled X.

"My question exactly!" retorted Y.

There was a long, tense silence. Then Y announced dramatically: "I've been living a lie! Every night I undo the day's repairs. I do not want to leave Wontoo and its merry madcaps!"

"Why, that is my confession as well!" gasped X. "I've come to love this land—its straight roads, tidy homes, and excellent lecture series."

"Do you think we've 'gone native'?" asked Y tentatively.

"I certainly hope so!" rejoined X, clapping him on the back.

They celebrated their mutual joy by breaking into dance. (I'll let you guess who did a wild fandango and who performed a sedate two-step.)

Happily, our story does not end here. This is what happened: Y and X did repair their Aerocycle, and it went on permanent display at the Wontooi National Aerocycle Museum. X and Y each married, very happily, and had many children and grandchildren. One was a dedicatedly doting grandpa. One was a wonderfully wild one.